TAURUS:

A COMPLETE GUIDE TO THE TAURUS ASTROLOGY STAR SIGN

Sofia Visconti

Contents

INTRODUCTION

Throughout history, humans have always looked up at the night sky with a sense of wonder and curiosity. For centuries astrology has been a trusted companion, offering insights into our personalities, relationships and the mysteries of life. At its essence astrology is based on the belief that celestial bodies like planets and stars have an influence on affairs and natural phenomena through their positions and movements.

The zodiac acts as a map of astrology consisting of twelve signs that provide a framework for understanding the distinct qualities and tendencies associated with individuals born under each sign. Each astrological sign possesses its own characteristics, strengths and obstacles. Astrologers use the study of these signs to provide guidance and promote self awareness. Astrology serves as a tool in navigating the landscapes of life, relationships and personal development.

In this book we embark on an exploration of one constellation within the zodiac; Taurus. As we delve into the realm of astrology and explore the Taurus sign we'll uncover a wealth of knowledge spanning history, mythology, psychology, personal development and much more. Our exploration will encompass understanding the personalities, strengths and challenges that define those born under this sign. By gaining insights into Taurus individuals both within ourselves and in our relationships we can foster a complete understanding.

Whether you are a follower of astrology or simply curious about it, our journey through the realm of Taurus promises to be both enlightening and enriching. This book aspires to equip you with knowledge that empowers self awareness while cultivating an appreciation for how cosmic influences shape our existence. As we embark on this journey together let us open our minds and hearts to the realm of Taurus that lies ahead.

OVERVIEW THE TAURUS ZODIAC SIGN

- **Date**; Taurus season starts from April 20th and extends until May 20th, marking a time of the year where the spring is in full bloom in the northern hemisphere. It is a time when the earth starts to show its bountifulness, symbolizing the Taurus traits of growth and stability.

- **Symbol**; The Bull, representing Taurus, symbolizes strength, tenacity, and a grounded nature.
- **Element**; As an Earth sign, Taurus is deeply connected to the physical world and material things. This element represents solidity, stability, and practicality.
- **Planet**; Ruled by Venus, the planet of love, beauty, and money. Taurus individuals often have an appreciation for art, aesthetics, and the pleasures of the senses..
- **Color**; Green, symbolizing growth, harmony and the beauty of the world. It also reflects their connection to the earth's abundance.
- **Traits**; Taurus, is often associated with stability, practicality and a strong connection to the world. Individuals born under this sign are recognized for their determination and resolute nature.

STRENGTHS

- **Reliability**; Taureans are renowned for their reliability and they can be relied upon to honor their commitments.
- **Determination**; Once a Taurus sets their sights on a goal they pursue it with determination.
- **Practicality**; Taurus possess a sense of practicality and approaches life's challenges with grounded perspectives.
- **Sensuality**; Being ruled by Venus, the planet of love and beauty, Taureans often have an

appreciation for life's pleasures and aesthetic delights.

- **Loyalty**; Taureans have a sense of loyalty, towards their friends and loved ones forming lasting bonds.

WEAKNESSES

- **Stubbornness**; Taurus individuals can be quite stubborn and resistant to change often preferring the comfort of what they know.
- **Possessiveness**; They may tend to be possessive in relationships valuing security and stability in their connections.
- **Materialism**; Their affection for the material world can sometimes lean towards materialism placing importance on possessions.
- **Resistance to Change**; Taurus individuals can be hesitant when it comes to embracing change, which might result in missed opportunities for growth.
- **Indulgence**; Their sensual nature can occasionally lead them to overindulge in food, luxury or other pleasures.
- **Compatibility**; Taurus is known to have compatibility with earth signs like Virgo and Capricorn as well as water signs such as Cancer, Scorpio and Pisces. These signs often share values and priorities in relationships and life.

In essence individuals born under Taurus are characterized by stability and practicality. They bring reliability and determination to their endeavors while being driven by a rooted desire for security and sensuality.

In the beginning of our exploration, into the Taurus zodiac sign we set off on an adventure through the realm of astrology, where it is believed that the positions of celestial bodies have an impact on human affairs. We discovered that Taurus, represented by the steadfast bull, holds a unique position in this tapestry. Now we will delve further into the realm of Taurus in an attempt to unlock its secrets and unravel its mysteries. Our journey will transport us across time and cultures as we explore the origins and mythical tales surrounding Taurus. We will also delve into the personalities, strengths and weaknesses exhibited by those born under this sign. By doing so, we aim to offer insights into both Taurus individuals who are part of our lives and our own self discovery. Our goal is to empower you with knowledge, self awareness and a profound appreciation for the influences that shape our existence. So dear reader join us as we turn the pages and delve deeper into the world of Taurus.

CHAPTER 1:
HISTORY AND MYTHOLOGY

In the realm of astrology each zodiac sign carries a tapestry of history, mythology and symbolism. Among these entities Taurus, symbolized by the steadfast bull stands strong. In this chapter we embark on a journey, through time and culture to explore the narratives and mythological tales that surround the Taurus sign.

Taurus has inspired humanity for centuries as it occupies a prominent position in the zodiac. From ancient civilizations like Mesopotamia and Egypt to the worlds of Greece and Rome, the bull has always held great significance in our collective imagination.

As we dive into the history and mythology surrounding Taurus we will uncover stories about seduction, seasonal changes and the profound connection between phenomena and earthly affairs. We will explore how ancient civilizations interpreted Taurus mythologically while reflecting on how this celestial entity shaped their beliefs and practices.

Furthermore our exploration will include an examination of how perceptions and understandings of Taurus have evolved over time. The transition, from interpreting Taurus through mythology to gaining personal insights has expanded our understanding of this constellation. Without further ado, join us on a journey through time as we delve into the enduring impact of Taurus in history and mythology.

EARLIEST OBSERVATIONS OF TAURUS

Dating back thousands of years, ancient civilizations such as the Mesopotamians, Egyptians and Greeks recorded their observations of the Taurus constellation. These ancient cultures gazed at the night sky and identified patterns among the stars while attributing cultural significance to them.

MESOPOTAMIA

Considered by many as the cradle of civilization, Mesopotamia associated the Taurus constellation with Marduk, their god. In star maps, the mighty deity was often portrayed as a divine bull. This representation symbolized strength and fertility. Moreover the positioning of this constellation in the night sky played an important role in agriculture and calendars. Its appearance marked the arrival of spring. A time for sowing seeds and beginning cycles.

ANCIENT GREECE

The Ancient Greeks assimilated elements of Egyptian astronomy into their understanding of the night sky. In Greek Mythology Taurus is closely linked to the tale of Europa and the Bull. According to this myth Europa, a princess from Phoenicia encountered a bull while picking flowers near the sea. Unbeknownst to her this bull was none other than Zeus himself disguised as a creature. Europa was captivated by the nature of the bull so she decided to climb onto its back. Taking advantage of the opportunity Zeus swiftly whisked her away, to Crete, an island filled with enchantment and mystery. This ancient myth holds symbolism exploring themes of abduction, transformation and the divine essence found within the Taurus constellation. It highlights how the bull represents power and sensuality, Zeus attempt to seduce Europa.

ANCIENT EGYPT

In Ancient Egypt, the Taurus constellation was linked to Hathor, their goddess who was often depicted with cow horns. Hathor personified love, music, fertility and motherhood. The presence of Taurus in the sky correlated with events like flooding of the Nile River. This was an important event for agriculture and civilization. Its connection reinforced the bulls association with abundance and prosperity.

MODERN ASTROLOGY

The Taurus constellation contains objects such as the Hyades star cluster and the Pleiades star cluster, which continue to captivate astronomers and stargazers alike. To sum up, the Taurus constellation boasts a diverse history that traces back to ancient civilizations observations and interpretations. Over time it has been linked with fertility, mythology and seasonal changes contributing to humanity's tapestry and our ongoing fascination with the wonders of the night sky.

Throughout mythologies Taurus, represented by the bull, encompasses a multitude of symbolic meanings such, as strength, fertility, sensuality and transformation. This constellation holds importance as it served as a marker for seasonal events due to its prominent position in the night sky. While specific myths and interpretations varied among cultures Taurus remained a celestial entity that influenced the beliefs and practices of these ancient civilizations.

The perception and understanding of Taurus has undergone significant changes throughout history. In ancient civilizations Taurus was often associated with concepts like fertility, agriculture and the cyclical nature of seasons. In modern astrology there has been a transition away from relying on mythological interpretations of zodiac signs, towards incorporating psychological insights into personality analysis. Taurus is now frequently linked to personality traits such as determination, stability and an appreciation for life.

NOTABLE HISTORICAL EVENTS UNDER "TAURUS"

Throughout history various significant events have occurred during the period associated with Taurus. It is important to note that astrology lacks proof; however some individuals believe that celestial alignments may influence affairs. During the Taurus season some notable events took place, each with its potential astrological significance.

- **The Signing of the United States Declaration of Independence (May 1776)**; The signing of the Declaration of Independence occurred during the Taurus season. This document holds importance as it symbolizes determination and resilience. Both are known traits of Taurus.

- **The End of World War II in Europe (May 1945);** The surrender of Nazi Germany coincided with the Taurus season marking the conclusion of World War II in Europe. This event can be seen as a transition towards a peaceful era aligning with the stability often linked to Taurus.

- **Apollo 11 Moon Landing (May 1969);** Neil Armstrong and Buzz Aldrin's historic moon landing happened during the Taurus season. This remarkable achievement showcased beauty and aesthetics which are connected to Venus, the ruling planet of Taurus.

Additionally there have been notable historical figures born under the sign of Taurus. While astrology cannot definitively explain their impact, some believe that certain personality traits attributed to Taurus may have contributed to their success.

- **William Shakespeare (April 23 1564)**; This renowned playwright and poet is widely regarded as one of the most famous writers ever. His works have had a lasting impact on literature and culture.

- **Karl Marx (May 5 1818)**; Known as a philosopher and political theorist Marx's ideas have profoundly influenced political thought through Marxism.

For those who want to delve further into the historical and mythological aspects of Taurus, below is a list of primary sources, ancient texts and contemporary writings.

Ancient Texts and Sources;

- **"The Epic of Gilgamesh"**- An ancient Mesopotamian epic that explores celestial events of significance including the prominent role played by the constellation Taurus.
- **"Metamorphoses"** by Ovid - A Roman narrative poem that includes the captivating myth of Europa and the Bull. This tale significantly contributes to our understanding of Taurus.
- "The Pyramid Texts". - An Ancient Egyptian religious text discovered within the pyramids that mentions Taurus.

Modern Writings on Astrology and Taurus;

- **"The Only Astrology Book You'll Ever Need"** by Joanna Martine Woolfolk. A comprehensive work that provides insights into Taurus personalities and astrological interpretations.
- **"The Secret Language of Birthdays"** by Gary Goldschneider and Joost Elffers. A resource offering personality profiles, for each zodiac sign, including a rich exploration of Taurus.

CHAPTER 2: LOVE & COMPATIBILITY

In the world of astrology the Taurus zodiac sign is known for its blend of sensuality, loyalty and unwavering determination. Nowhere do these traits shine brighter, than in matters of the heart. In this chapter we embark on an exploration of how Taurus approaches love and compatibility with other signs of the zodiac.

Love, which is universally understood as the language of the heart, takes on a unique flavor when experienced by individuals born under the Taurus sign. Their steadfast commitment, kind nature and appreciation for life weaves together to form a unique tapestry of love. As we delve into the world of Taurus individuals we will explore their unwavering loyalty in matters of love.

Furthermore we will venture into the intricacies of how Taurus pairs up with other zodiac signs by examining their challenges faced together. In addition to the potential strengths that arise when these celestial energies intertwine. Whether you're a Taurus looking to understand your tendencies or someone curious about the Taurus in your life this chapter offers an exploration of love and compatibility.

LOVE LANGUAGE OF TAURUS

The way Taurus approaches love and romance is characterized by an appreciation for sensuality, loyalty and a strong desire for stability in relationships. Taurus individuals embrace love with genuine intentions and practicality. Here is more on how Taurus approaches love.

- **Stability and Security;** Stability and security hold high value, for individuals born under the sign of Taurus when it comes to relationships. They seek partners who can provide them with a sense of safety and dependability. Once they commit to a relationship they are typically committed for the long term. As such they are willing to invest time and effort into making it thrive.

- **Sensuality and Passion**; Taurus individuals, ruled by Venus, the planet associated with love and beauty possess an inclination towards sensuality and physical pleasures. They often express their affection through touch. Romance holds a significance for Taurus individuals as it captivates all of their senses.

- **Loyalty and Devotion**; Known for their loyalty Taurus individuals exhibit unwavering commitment once they fall in love. They become partners who are willing to go to great lengths to support and safeguard their loved ones.
- **Practicality in Love**; When it comes to matters of the heart Taurus individuals approach love with practicality. They don't rush into relationships. Rather they take their time to evaluate the compatibility with potential partners and examine the long term prospects of the relationship.
- **Material Comfort**; The connection Taurus has with the material world sometimes translates into a desire for creature comforts. They appreciate gifts as tokens of affection. Often they enjoy sharing these delights with their partners. However it's important to note that their inclination towards materialism is often driven by creating a cozy environment for their loved ones.
- **Conflict Avoidance**; In relationships Taurus individuals tend to steer clear of conflict or unnecessary drama. They have a preference for maintaining harmony and peace. They possess the skill to find compromises and solutions when disagreements arise. However their occasional stubbornness can lead to prolonged disagreements if their core values are challenged.

In summary Taurus individuals approach love and romance with a focus on stability, sensuality, loyalty and practicality. As such they seek partners who can offer security and create a sense of home. Although they may be cautious in matters of love, once they commit to someone they wholeheartedly invest themselves in building enduring and fulfilling relationships based on trust, comfort and deep emotional connections with their partners.

COMPATIBILITY BETWEEN TAURUS AND OTHER ZODIAC SIGNS

TAURUS AND ARIES

These two signs exhibit notable differences. Taurus is known for being patient and valuing stability. Aries tends to be adventurous and values independence. Taurus might perceive Aries as hasty or impulsive. Aries may view Taurus as boring. However if both partners can recognize each other's strengths they can find common ground. Communicating effectively their differences, they can actually work together in a complementary way.

TAURUS AND TAURUS

Of course these two have key similarities such as a shared love for stability, sensuality and material comforts. They both highly value loyalty and are partners who create a strong bond. However their stubbornness might occasionally cause conflicts because they both resist change. In such situations, patience and understanding become crucial in resolving any disputes that arise.

TAURUS AND GEMINI

Taurus individuals tend to be grounded and practical in their approach to life and relationships. On the other hand Geminis are known for being curious and adaptable. This fundamental difference might make it challenging for Taurus to deal with Gemini's unpredictability or need for variety. Meanwhile Gemini may perceive Taurus as too focused on routines. A successful relationship between these signs requires compromise from both sides along with an appreciation of each other's qualities.

TAURUS AND CANCER

This is considered a strong pairing due to their shared values of emotional connection, family bonds and security. Taurus brings stability along with practicality to the relationship. Cancer offers depth well as nurturing qualities. Together they create a foundation based on understanding. Their shared desire for a secure home life can foster a long lasting relationship.

TAURUS AND LEO

Taurus and Leo have varying approaches to life and love. Taurus seeks stability and security while Leo craves attention and admiration. Taurus might feel overwhelmed by Leo's need for the spotlight. Leo might perceive Taurus as overly cautious. Building a successful relationship would involve finding a balance between meeting Leo's need for recognition and fulfilling Taurus' desire for stability.

TAURUS AND VIRGO

This pairing is highly compatible as both signs share a nature of practicality and a fondness for paying attention to details. Taurus appreciates Virgo's mindset and nurturing qualities while Virgo admires Tauruss reliability and stability. Their shared values along with their dedication to each other can result in a bond that stands the test of time.

TAURUS AND LIBRA

There are some noticeable differences between Taurus and Libra. Taurus values practicality and stability. Libra emphasizes harmony and fairness. Taurus may perceive Libra as indecisive while Libra might see Taurus as rigid. Open communication along with willingness to compromise is crucial in order to find common ground that leads to a balanced relationship.

TAURUS AND SCORPIO

The connection between Taurus and Scorpio can be intense and passionate because both signs deeply desire intimacy. Tauruss stability complements the intensity of Scorpio while Scorpios loyalty aligns with Tauruss values. However it is important to note that both signs have a tendency to be possessive. Trust and open communication are vital in order to avoid issues related to jealousy and control.

TAURUS AND SAGITTARIUS

Taurus and Sagittarius approaches to life differ significantly. Taurus seeks stability in life. Sagittarius craves adventure and freedom. Taurus may perceive Sagittarius as spontaneous and unreliable while Sagittarius might view Taurus as overly cautious. In order for their relationship to thrive, understanding each other's perspectives and finding a compromise becomes essential.

TAURUS AND CAPRICORN

Compatibility between these two is quite high. Both signs share a love for stability, practicality and long term goals. Taurus appreciates Capricorn's ambition and determination. Capricorn highly values the loyalty and reliability of Taurus. Their shared values create a foundation for a lasting partnership.

TAURUS WITH AQUARIUS

Taurus with Aquarius exhibit varying approaches towards life and love. Taurus cherishes tradition and security. Aquarius seeks innovation and independence. This divergence may lead to challenges in their relationship. Taurus might find Aquarius too unconventional while Aquarius could perceive Taurus as too traditional. Building a relationship often involves finding a common ground between these different perspectives.

TAURUS AND PISCES

This combination can be quite harmonious since both signs value connection, sensitivity and a feeling of security. Taurus offers practicality and stability. Pisces brings creativity and emotional depth to the relationship. However there may be instances where Taurus practical nature clashes with Pisces disposition. In such cases open communication and understanding become crucial.

To summarize the compatibility between Taurus and other zodiac signs varies depending on how they understand, appreciate and balance their differences. While astrology can provide insights into compatibility, individual personalities and experiences also play roles in determining the success of any relationship.

RELATIONSHIPS WITH TAURUS INDIVIDUALS

Taurus individuals are renowned for their dependability, sensuality and loyalty when it comes to relationships. Whether you're currently dating or in a relationship with a Taurus here are some tips for both men and women.

TIPS FOR A RELATIONSHIP WITH A TAURUS MAN

- **Reliability;** Appreciate the reliability of Taurus men in your life whether its support or emotional stability.
- **Aspire;** Share your hopes and dreams with them as they appreciate partners who open up about their aspirations.
- **Cultivate Patience;** Taurus men value taking their time when making decisions. Therefore it's important to avoid rushing them into commitments or pushing for changes in the relationship. Give them space to feel comfortable and secure.
- **Show Your Appreciation;** Taurus men love feeling valued. Let them know that you admire their qualities and efforts. This will boost their confidence and strengthen your bond.
- **Be Patient with Their Stubbornness;** Taurus men can be quite stubborn at times. When confronting them, try to find common ground and compromise when disagreements arise.
- **Share Your Emotions;** Although Taurus men may not always openly express their feelings they

appreciate it when their partners do so. Share your emotions with them. Create a space for vulnerability.

- **Respect Their Need for Routine;** Taurus men often value routines as they provide stability and predictability in their lives. Be understanding of this need. Support them in maintaining it.
- **Respect Their Need for Space;** Personal space holds significance for Taurus individuals; they cherish moments of solitude as an opportunity to recharge. It is vital to understand that their need for time should not be interpreted as rejection but as an essential aspect of who they are.

TIPS FOR A RELATIONSHIP WITH A TAURUS WOMAN

- **Celebrate Special Moments;** Taurus women enjoy celebrations and meaningful gestures. Remember dates, such as anniversaries or birthdays. Make an effort to celebrate them with thoughtful gifts or shared experiences.
- **Appreciate Their Loyalty;** Taurus women are partners who stand by your side through thick and thin. Show gratitude for their support making sure they understand how much you value their commitment.
- **Demonstrate Consistency;** Winning a Tauruss heart requires showcasing reliability and consistency. Ensure that you keep your promises arrive punctually and establish yourself as someone they can rely on.

- **Freedom;** Avoid being overly possessive or controlling as Taurus women value their independence and personal interests.
- **Delight Their Senses;** Since Taurus people possess an affinity for the material world indulging their senses can be particularly enchanting. Plan romantic outings that cater to their pleasures—think dining experiences, soothing massages or cozy movie nights at home.
- **Foster Trust;** Trust forms the bedrock of any relationship with a Taurus person. Thus it is crucial to maintain honesty and open communication at all times since even the slightest hint of dishonesty can undermine their trust in the relationship.

These guidelines will assist you in strengthening a connection with your Taurus partner. Keep in mind that while these tips can offer guidance every person is unique. A successful relationship with a Taurus individual like any other relies on communication, understanding and mutual respect. Love isn't solely determined by one zodiac sign. Rather it encompasses how different energies interact between individuals.

In wrapping up the chapter we have explored the aspects of love and compatibility within the Taurus zodiac sign. Throughout this chapter we have delved into how Taurus individuals approach matters of the heart and examined the complexities of their preferences. From their sensuality, to their loyalty Taurus individuals bring a beautiful blend of love into their relationships. They appreciate the comforts that life has to offer and place value on the security and stability that love provides. Their ability to create a harmonious environment along with their dedication to their partners makes them cherished companions in the journey of love.

CHAPTER 3: FRIENDS AND FAMILY

In the tapestry of life our connections with friends and family play an important role weaving together to create a mosaic of our existence. For those who are born under the Taurus zodiac sign these relationships bring their qualities of loyalty, stability and sensuality to the forefront. This chapter takes us on an exploration of how Taurus individuals approach friendships and family dynamics.

Taurus individuals offer a constant and reliable presence, in the lives of those they hold dear. However, like any zodiac sign, they encounter unique challenges when it comes to relationships. In this discussion we will delve into these challenges in order to better understand how to navigate them and foster healthier and more harmonious connections. Join us on this journey as we delve into the connections that define the Taurus experience within the realm of friends and family.

TAURUS AS A FRIEND

Taurus individuals are friends who can be relied upon. Just as they are renowned for their loyalty, in relationships their steadfast and trustworthy nature also extends to their friendships. Here's what you can anticipate when you have a Taurus as a friend.

- **Loyalty**; Taurus friends exhibit loyalty. They will stand by your side through thick and thin consistently offering support when you need it most. Their loyalty is unwavering, making them trusted companions.
- **Dependability**; When it comes to reliability Taurus friends are unmatched. They are individuals who will never leave you hanging in any situation. When Taurus individuals promise to be there, they genuinely mean it.
- **Stability**; People born under the Taurus zodiac sign highly value stability and have a knack for bringing a sense of calmness to their friendships. They are the anchors in your life providing support and a feeling of security.

- **Generosity**; Taurus friends are known for their generous nature. Often they find much joy in sharing life's pleasures with their companions. Whether it's treating you to a meal or presenting gifts they express their affection through acts of generosity.

- **Attentive Listeners**; Taurus individuals make great listeners. They exhibit patience and attentiveness when you need someone to talk to. They create a non-judgmental space where you can freely share your thoughts and emotions.

- **Appreciation for Sensory Delights**; Taurus friends often possess an appreciation for sensory pleasures like delicious food, music and relaxation. They can introduce you to experiences or help you relish life's simple joys.

- **Conflict Resolution Skills**; While Taurus friends prefer harmony they also excel at resolving conflicts. They approach problem solving with practicality and groundedness which proves beneficial when issues arise.

- **Honesty**; Honesty and trust hold significance for Taurus individuals, in their friendships. You can count on them to provide advice while keeping your confidence intact.

- **Shared Bonds**; Taurus friends often find joy in establishing and sharing traditions and routines. Whether it's a movie night, a getaway or other shared activities they value the continuity and connection that arise from these experiences.

Although Taurus friends possess qualities that enrich your life it's worth noting that their determination can occasionally lead to disagreements. Nevertheless their loyalty and dedication to the friendship usually help overcome such challenges. If you have a Taurus friend, treasure the stability and steadfast support they provide.

FAMILY

Taurus individuals contribute key qualities and dynamics to family life. Their strong sense of stability, loyalty and practicality typically influence relationships and interactions. Let's take a closer look at how Taurus influences family dynamics.

- **Stability**; Like the oak tree in the family forest, Taurus serves as a reliable foundation for their loved ones. They are key members of the family often playing the role of the anchor that keeps the family grounded.
- **Loyalty**; Taurus individuals exhibit loyalty, towards their family. They develop long lasting bonds with their parents, siblings and extended relatives. Family gatherings and traditions hold great importance to them as they cherish the feeling of unity and belonging they bring.
- **Caring and Protective**; Taurus individuals often take on a nurturing role within their family. They naturally gravitate towards caring for children and elderly members displaying a nurturing and protective nature. Creating a harmonious home environment brings them much joy.
- **Appreciation for Comfort**; Taurus individuals have an affinity for material comforts, which is

reflected in their desire to create a cozy and visually appealing home. Providing their family with a sense of security in an inviting atmosphere is something they truly enjoy.

- **Embracing Tradition**; Taurus individuals value family values highly. Family dinners, celebrations and customs hold significance for them. Family traditions and routines play a role in their lives as they provide continuity and foster connection.

- **Promoting Harmony**; Taurus individuals prioritize maintaining harmony within the family unit often taking on the role of peacemaker during conflicts. They approach conflict resolution by emphasizing compromise and seeking ground.

- **Generosity**; Taurus is known for their generous nature especially when it comes to their family. They willingly provide support or lend a helping hand whenever their loved ones need it. They often take charge in organizing family get-togethers. There they ensure that everyone's well being is taken care of.

- **Parenting Style**; When it comes to being parents Taurus individuals are nurturing. They create a secure environment for their children emphasizing the importance of responsibility and practical life skills.

- **Cherished Family Traditions;** Family traditions hold significance for Taurus. Whether it's celebrating holidays, hosting family reunions or passing down treasured heirlooms they actively preserve the legacy of family history and customs.

- **Maintaining Family Bonds;** Taurus recognizes the importance of keeping connections alive with family members. They make efforts to nurture relationships with aunts, uncles, cousins and other relatives fostering a sense of unity within the family.

While Tauruss positive qualities greatly contribute to family dynamics it is essential to acknowledge that their stubbornness can sometimes lead to disagreements due to resistance towards change or strong opinions within the family. However the loyalty and dedication that Taurus individuals possess towards their family bonds often enable them to overcome difficulties. This fosters a sense of unity and security that is deeply cherished by their loved ones.

CHALLENGES IN RELATIONSHIPS WITH FAMILY AND FRIENDS

Although Taurus individuals bring qualities to their friendships and family relationships they may also face specific challenges due to their inherent traits and tendencies. Here are some common hurdles that Taurus individuals might encounter.

- **Stubbornness**; Taurus individuals are renowned for their determination and unwavering resolve. While this can be an asset it can sometimes manifest as stubbornness. They might be resistant to change or unwilling to consider perspectives leading to conflicts and strained relationships. This aspect of their personality can pose challenges in relationships that require adaptability. As such they may struggle with transitions or exhibit reluctance towards new experiences. Meeting others halfway can be a way forward.
- **Possessiveness**; Tauruss loyalty and desire for security can occasionally result in possessiveness within friendships and family ties. They may become overly protective of their loved ones, which can feel suffocating and restrict growth.
- **Materialism**; Due to their connection with the material world and affinity for material comforts, Taurus individuals might occasionally develop an emphasis on possessions. This might be misunderstood, as materialism by friends and family which could potentially cause tensions regarding priorities.

- **Apathy**; Taurus individuals can find it challenging to express their emotions. They tend to be reserved when it comes to sharing their feelings, which can be frustrating for loved ones who desire connection and communication.

- **Avoidance**; While Taurus desire for harmony is a trait it can sometimes lead to avoiding conflicts. They may suppress their emotions. Avoid addressing issues within relationships in order to maintain peace resulting in unresolved conflicts.

- **Hesitance**; Taurus individuals may hesitate to seek help or advice when it's necessary. They prefer solving problems which can lead to prolonged issues or missed opportunities for growth.

- **Overindulgence**; Their fondness for pleasures and comfort sometimes leads them to overindulgence – whether it's overindulging in food, luxury items or other pleasures. These factors can have a negative impact on their well being. It can also strain their relationships with concerned individuals.

- **Slow to Forgive**; Taurus people tend to hold grudges or harbor resentments for a long time. Their reluctance to forgive and move on can hinder the process of healing in relationships and perpetuate negativity.

It's worth noting that these challenges are not impossible to overcome and Taurus individuals can develop strategies to address them. Being self aware, maintaining communication and being willing to adapt are crucial in overcoming these challenges. Additionally the support and understanding from friends and family members can play a role in helping Taurus individuals navigate these dynamics effectively.

In the dance of life Taurus individuals serve as pillars of stability steadfastly devoted to their loved ones. In this chapter we have delved into the realm of Taurus friendships and family dynamics discovering the influence they have on the lives of those enough to be part of their circle.

As friends Taurus individuals bring unwavering loyalty, reliable support and a deep appreciation for life's pleasures, into their relationships. They are the ones you can rely on through thick and thin forging bonds that endure the trials of time.

Within a family Taurus individuals play a role, as a pillar of tradition, stability and unwavering commitment. They highly value family gatherings, cherished traditions and the comforting atmosphere of home that fosters the growth and prosperity of each generation.

However just like any aspect of life, friendships and family relationships present their share of challenges. Tauruss willed nature, resistance to change and occasional possessiveness can sometimes create hurdles in maintaining harmony. It is essential to acknowledge these challenges with empathy and engage in communication to address them effectively.

As we wrap up this chapter let's keep in mind that Taurus individuals bring a combination of stability, loyalty and sensuality to their relationships, with friends and family. By recognizing their strengths and challenges and by nurturing empathetic connections Taurus individuals can build lasting, meaningful and harmonious relationships that enhance both their own lives and the lives of those they care about.

CHAPTER 4:
CAREER AND AMBITIONS

When it comes to careers and finances, Taurus individuals truly stand out as reliable and hardworking professionals. They bring a hard working ethic, a commitment to excellence and a keen focus on security. In this chapter we delve into the connection between Taurus individuals, their career aspirations and how they handle money matters.

For Taurus individuals choosing a career is not just about earning a living; it's also an expression of their values and desires. The pursuit of stability, financial security and practicality significantly influences the path they choose in their lives. Known for their determination, meticulous attention to detail and unwavering dedication to their work, Taurus individuals thrive in various fields.

As we delve into the realm of Taurus and their ambitions, in the professional spheres we'll gain an understanding of their unique qualities and the values that shape their choices in the world of work and money. So dear reader, come along as we explore how individuals with the Taurus star sign approach their careers and finances.

CAREER ASPIRATIONS

Taurus individuals tackle their careers with determination, practicality and steadfastness. Furthermore they have distinct preferences and aspirations that reflect their distinctive personality traits. Now let's take a closer look at Tauruss career inclinations and professional goals.

- **Stability**; Taurus individuals hold stability and financial security in high regard when it comes to their careers. They are drawn to professions that offer a steady income stream with long term prospects.
- **Practicality**; Individuals with Taurus traits possess an inclination towards practicality and realism. Often they gravitate towards careers that align with these tendencies, such as finance, accounting, real estate or healthcare. They excel in

roles that demand attention to detail along with a pragmatic approach.

- **Materialism**; People born under the Taurus zodiac sign have an admiration for the material world, which often influences their career choices towards fields related to assets. They may find fulfillment in professions involving luxury goods, fashion, interior design or culinary arts.
- **Nurture**; Given their nurturing side Taurus individuals are well suited for professions that involve caring for others and making an impact on people's lives. This makes them suitable for careers in healthcare, education or caregiving.
- **Creativity**; Due to their appreciation of beauty and sensory pleasures many Tauruses are drawn towards creative outlets. They may choose careers in art, music, theater or design where they can express their talents and create pleasing experiences.
- **Patience**; Tauruses tend to make progress at a steady pace, rather than rushing things. They exhibit patience and hold the belief that hard work and determination will ultimately lead to success.
- **Prudence**; Financial prudence is another trait commonly found among Taurus individuals. They prioritize saving and investing aligning with their term goals and desire for security.

To summarize, Taurus individuals are attracted to careers that offer stability, financial security and the chance to work with assets or in nurturing roles. Their practicality, patience and dedication make them valuable contributors across many fields. While they excel in some roles. Finding a balance between their resistance to change and potential for growth is a consideration on their journey.

STRENGTHS THAT MAKE TAURUS INDIVIDUALS STAND OUT IN THE WORKPLACE

- **Reliability**; Taurus individuals are well known for their reliability. When they make a commitment you can trust them to follow through. This characteristic is highly valued in work settings because colleagues and supervisors can rely on them to keep their promises and meet deadlines consistently.
- **Strong Work Ethic**; Taurus individuals have a dedication to their work. They are willing to put in the necessary effort to excel in their roles. They approach tasks with determination and persistence often going above and beyond to achieve results.
- **Attention to Detail**; Their meticulous attention to detail is an asset in professions that require precision and accuracy. Taurus individuals shine in roles that involve data analysis, quality control, research or any task that demands an eye for specifics.
- **Practical Problem Solving**; Taurus individuals have a practical approach when it comes to solving problems. They excel at identifying challenges and finding solutions. Their down to earth perspective often leads to problem resolution.

- **Consistency**; Taurus individuals thrive in environments that offer stability and routine. They are well suited for roles that require consistency and the ability to handle tasks patiently and precisely. Their constant presence in the workplace contributes to creating a harmonious environment.

- **Perseverance**; Taurus individuals possess a sense of determination. When faced with obstacles or challenges they persistently work towards their goals making them valuable team members in projects that span over periods.

- **Financial Expertise**; Many Taurus individuals have a talent for financial matters. They excel in roles related to finance, accounting, budgeting and investments.

- **Organized**; Taurus individuals are often highly organized. They thrive in hierarchical environments where they can efficiently manage their tasks and responsibilities. Their organizational skills contribute to productivity and efficiency at work.

- **Conflict Resolution**; Taurus desire for harmony extends to their ability to handle conflicts. They approach disagreements with a calm demeanor while seeking compromises and solutions that maintain a harmonious work atmosphere.

- **Growth Perspective**; Taurus individuals typically have a long term outlook on their careers. They possess patience. Understand the value of steady progress. Taurus individuals with their commitment to achieving their goals often experience long term success and accomplishments.

COMMON CAREER CHALLENGES WITH STRATEGIES TO OVERCOME THEM

While Taurus individuals bring many strengths to the workplace it's important to acknowledge that they may also face challenges. By recognizing and addressing these challenges head on, Taurus individuals can truly thrive in their careers.

Resistance Towards Change

- Challenge; One of the traits of Taurus individuals is their resistance towards change due to a preference for stability and a familiar routine. This tendency might hinder adaptability in paced or rapidly evolving work environments.
- Strategy; To overcome this challenge it is beneficial for Taurus individuals to gradually embrace change. By exposing themselves consistently to novel experiences they can build confidence in adapting to unfamiliar situations.

Stubbornness

- Challenge; Sometimes Taurus individuals' determination and strong opinions can make it difficult for them to collaborate with others or consider other viewpoints.
- Strategy; Taurus individuals can work on being more open minded, by listening to other perspectives and being open to feedback.

Engaging in discussions and being willing to compromise can lead to more harmonious work relationships.

Risk Aversion

- Challenge; Taurus individuals often prioritize security and may be hesitant to take calculated risks or explore career paths.
- Strategy; While it is important to maintain stability Taurus individuals can assess the benefits of calculated risks and consider exploring new career opportunities. Gradually introduce calculated risks into career plans allowing them to explore opportunities without jeopardizing their security.

Overemphasis on Materialism

- Challenge; Tauruss strong affinity for the material world may result in a focus on rewards potentially overshadowing other aspects of career satisfaction.
- Strategy; Taurus individuals should strive for a balance between security and overall career fulfillment. By identifying roles or projects that align with their passions and values they can find job satisfaction, beyond considerations.

Resistance, to Changing Careers

- Challenge; Taurus individuals often find themselves getting comfortable in their roles because they prefer stability.
- Strategy; To overcome this challenge Taurus individuals can set career goals and regularly

evaluate whether their current position aligns with their aspirations and values. Seeking guidance from mentors, expanding their network and considering alternative career paths can offer fresh perspectives.

Hesitation in Pursuing Advancement

- Challenge; Tauruss patient and determined nature sometimes results in a reluctance to actively pursue career advancement or seek promotions.
- Strategy; Taurus individuals can address this challenge by communicating their career objectives to supervisors and actively seeking opportunities for skill enhancement and upward mobility within the organization. Building connections can also open doors to new possibilities.

Persevering Despite Discontentment

- Challenge; Tauruss persevering nature may cause them to persist in a career that no longer brings them satisfaction or fulfillment.
- Strategy; Taurus individuals should periodically assess their level of job satisfaction. Take action if they find themselves in unfulfilling roles. Exploring options such as career counseling, mentorship programs or further education can assist them in aligning their careers with their passions and aspirations.

Throughout this chapter we have explored the relationship that Taurus individuals have with their aspirations and approach to wealth. For them, careers go beyond the grind. They are a reflection of their core values. Their pursuit of stability, financial security and a comfortable life underlies their choices. They are professionals who pay attention to detail and excel. Their natural financial acumen, discipline and ability to plan for the term serve them well in building a brighter future.

As we wrap up this chapter we hope you now have a good understanding of how Taurus individuals approach career growth and money. Ultimately Taurus people serve as a reminder that success goes beyond the amount of money in your bank account. It also encompasses the stability, security and satisfaction that comes from choosing a career you love.

CHAPTER 5: SELF-IMPROVEMENT

In the pursuit of discovering oneself and growing personally each zodiac sign possesses unique qualities and characteristics that shape their journey. For those born under the Taurus zodiac sign their path towards self improvement is defined by a commitment to stability, practicality and reliability. In this chapter we will explore how they can utilize their traits to become the best versions of themselves.

Taurus individuals are renowned for their hard work and affinity for materialistic pursuits. When it comes to self improvement they approach it with the determination they apply to their careers and finances. Their practical nature and steadfast loyalty to their values serve as guiding principles on their growth journey.

However, like individuals from all zodiac signs, Taurus faces both challenges and opportunities while striving for self improvement. Their resistance to change and occasional stubbornness can hinder progress. Within this chapter we will explore strategies and practices that can assist Taurus individuals in embracing self improvement. So my dear reader join us as we delve into the journey of Taurus individuals towards self improvement.

EMBRACING TAURUS STRENGTHS AND OVERCOMING WEAKNESSES

Taurus individuals possess a unique blend of strengths and weaknesses that shape their personality. To lead a fulfilling life it is crucial to leverage these strengths while working on areas that need improvement. Here's a helpful guide on achieving that.

UTILIZING STRENGTHS

- **Reliability**; Taurus reliability is an asset. Use it to establish trust in both professional and personal relationships. Keep your promises consistently through your actions.
- **Strong Work Ethic**; Make the most of your strong work ethic by excelling in your career

endeavors. Take on tasks, work diligently and strive for excellence. Your dedication will not go unnoticed.

- **Attention to Detail**; Your meticulous attention to detail can be advantageous, in roles that require precision. Consider exploring professions that involve working with data analysis, quality control or research. These fields can benefit greatly from your attention to detail. Focus on specifics.
- **Practical Problem Solving**; Your practical approach to problem solving is incredibly valuable. Use this skill to identify challenges, break them down into tasks and find solutions. Your practical mindset can lead to outcomes.
- **Consistency and Stability**; Embrace your preference for stability and routine. Establishing a routine can enhance productivity and reduce stress levels. Your consistency can bring comfort not only, to yourself but to those around you.

OVERCOMING WEAKNESSES

- **Resistance to Change**; While valuing stability is a strength it's important to acknowledge that change is a part of life. Practice flexibility by introducing experiences into your daily routine. Embrace change as an opportunity for growth.
- **Openness and Flexibility**; Work on being more receptive to perspectives by actively listening during discussions. Engage in conversations. Be willing to find compromises when necessary. An open minded approach leads to better interactions.

- **Managing Risk Aversion**; Challenge yourself by taking calculated risks both in your life. Start with small steps. Gradually increase your tolerance for risk taking activities. Understand that taking some level of risk is essential for growth and achieving success.

- **Developing oneself**; Growing as an individual is a journey that applies to Taurus individuals well. Embracing the qualities of being a Taurus, such as practicality and steadfastness while also being open to change and self improvement can lead to a satisfying and harmonious life.

- **Avoiding focus on possessions**; Although it's important to have comfort in life it's essential not to equate material things with happiness alone. Practicing gratitude and directing attention towards relationships, experiences and personal development can bring greater fulfillment.

- **Being open to career changes**; It's beneficial for Taurus individuals to periodically evaluate their career satisfaction levels and remain receptive to opportunities. Seeking guidance from mentors, networking with professionals from fields and considering education can broaden horizons.

- **Taking action - even when dissatisfied**; If you find yourself in an unfulfilling career situation taking action steps towards change is crucial. Exploring challenges, pursuing your passions and contemplating career paths are all worthwhile endeavors. Remember that pursuing long term happiness is always worth it.

By leveraging your strengths while actively working on areas that need improvement Taurus individuals can embark on a journey of growth and self improvement. This approach allows for a rewarding and successful life. Here are some more tips and growth strategies.

Take Change Slowly;

- Challenge for Taurus; Taurus individuals have a tendency to be resistant to change and prefer stability.
- Growth Approach; While it's important to maintain stability, try embracing change in steps. By exposing yourself to new experiences bit by bit you can become more adaptable over time.

Foster Open Mindedness;

- Challenge for Taurus; Stubbornness can sometimes hinder mindedness and flexibility.
- Growth Approach; Make an effort to genuinely listen to other perspectives and engage in discussions with an open heart and mind. Take the time to consider alternative viewpoints and be willing to adapt your beliefs when presented with new information.

Step Beyond Your Comfort Zone;

- Challenge for Taurus; Taurus individuals often stick within their routines and comfort zones.
- Growth Approach; Challenge yourself by trying out activities exploring interests or taking calculated risks. Stepping beyond your comfort zone can lead to growth. Broaden your horizons.

Set Ambitious Objectives;

- Challenge for Taurus; The love of stability may sometimes result in complacency or resistance towards setting goals.
- Growth Approach; Identify long term goals and aspirations both in your personal life. Create a plan on how you'll achieve them while remaining open, to adjusting those goals as you continue growing and evolving.

Developing Communication Skills;

- Challenge for Taurus; One challenge that Taurus individuals may face is the tendency to hold back their emotions or thoughts.
- Growth Approach; To overcome this challenge it is beneficial to practice assertive communication. Sharing your feelings, needs and opinions with your loved ones and colleagues can lead to relationships and personal growth.

Exploring Creativity;

- Challenge for Taurus; Another challenge for Taurus individuals is prioritizing practicality over self expression.
- Growth Approach; To nurture your side engage in activities such as art, music, writing or any other form of creative expression. Embracing your creativity can be a fulfilling experience.

Personal Development Opportunities;

- Challenge for Taurus; Taurus individuals may sometimes fall into complacency when it comes to growth.
- Growth Approach; To counter this challenge make an effort to seek opportunities for self improvement. Attend workshops, read books. Participate in activities that intellectually and emotionally challenge you.

Practicing Mindfulness and Patience;

- Challenge for Taurus; Taurus individuals may have a tendency to rush through life without appreciating the moment.
- Growth Approach; To cultivate mindfulness and patience in your life consider practicing gratitude exercises or engaging in meditation or yoga. These practices can help you stay present and enjoy the journey, rather than solely focusing on reaching your goals.

Maintaining a balance, between materialism and inner fulfillment;

- Challenge for Taurus; Sometimes being strongly connected to the material world can overshadow the importance of finding fulfillment.
- Growth Strategy; While it is important to have material comfort it is equally essential to prioritize well being, nurturing relationships and personal growth. Strive for a pursuit of both material goals and the pursuit of happiness and self discovery.

Ultimately personal growth involves embarking on a journey of self reflection, adapting to changes and continuously learning. Taurus individuals can leverage their strengths while working on their challenges in order to lead a life filled with fulfillment and personal development. By embracing change and remaining open to experiences, Taurus individuals can unlock their potential and achieve holistic personal growth.

As Taurus individuals contemplate their prospects, for growth and personal evolution it is important to remember that self improvement is a journey that unfolds gradually with purpose. There is endless potential for growth and self improvement among Taurus individuals. By embracing change, being open minded and stepping out of their comfort zones, Taurus individuals can unlock their full potential. This path is grounded in their determination and is guided by self awareness offering the promise of an enriched life.

CHAPTER 6:
THE YEAR AHEAD

As a Taurus your year ahead will be shaped by the changing cosmos, where celestial events influence the ups and downs of your life. This chapter acts as your guide to the stars. In the following pages we will explore dates and periods that hold significance. From Venus movements to solar eclipses we will uncover how these celestial happenings may affect your journey in the year ahead.

So dear Taurus, as you dive into this tapestry that awaits you in the year, always remember that the stars are here to guide you. Opportunities for growth and fulfillment are abundant like the universe itself. Embrace this journey. May the celestial energies align in your favor throughout the year.

HOROSCOPE GUIDE FOR TAURUS

Welcome, aboard Taurus! As you embark on your journey through the year there are promises of stability, personal growth and the potential to bring your dreams to life. Being an earth sign ruled by Venus, your practicality, determination and appreciation for life's pleasures are well known. This comprehensive yearly horoscope guide is designed to assist you in navigating the influences and making the most of what lies ahead.

- **January to March;** Evaluating priorities. The year commences with a focus on reevaluating your priorities regarding your career and relationships. Take some time to establish goals and lay a foundation for your endeavors. Trust your intuition when making decisions. <u>Be willing to let go of anything that no longer serves you.</u>

- **April to June;** Building financial security. During this period concentrate on building financial security while exploring opportunities for growth. Your practical nature and strong work ethic will guide you in making investments and financial choices. Consider long term goals. Set a plan in motion that includes saving.

- **July to September;** Broadening horizons. The months of the year encourage you to expand your horizons through travel, education or personal development. Embrace the new. Step out of your comfort zone. Seek inspiration, from cultures and perspectives as a means of widening your worldview.

- **October to December;** Strengthening connections. As the year comes to a close it's a time to strengthen your relationships whether it's with your partner or your family and friends. The key lies in communication and finding compromises when conflicts arise. Your loved ones will truly appreciate your loyalty and dedication.

- **Balance and Harmony**; Strive for balance in all areas of your life by taking care of yourself while pursuing your goals. It's important to nurture both your well being and aspirations.
- **Self Expression**; Explore your expressive side this year. Give voice to your inner thoughts and emotions. Engaging in creative activities can be particularly fulfilling.
- **Financial Growth**; Utilize your knowledge to secure a better financial future for yourself. Consider long term investments and savings plans that align with your goals.
- **Personal Growth**; Embrace change and personal development as you move forward. Don't shy away from experiences that push you out of your comfort zone. Keep a journal as a means of tracking progress on this journey of growth.
- **Reality**; Stay grounded in reality while trusting yourself and following your instincts.
- **Open mind**; Be open minded, adaptable and willing to adjust when faced with changing circumstances.
- **Nurture**; Prioritize self care to ensure both health and emotional well being. Nurture your relationships by being present, attentive and maintaining communication.

Remember, Taurus the stars are aligned in favor of opportunities, for growth, stability and personal fulfillment in the year! Have confidence in your abilities, embrace the opportunities for change and take pleasure in the joys of life. Your unwavering determination and practical approach will lead you towards success and fulfillment.

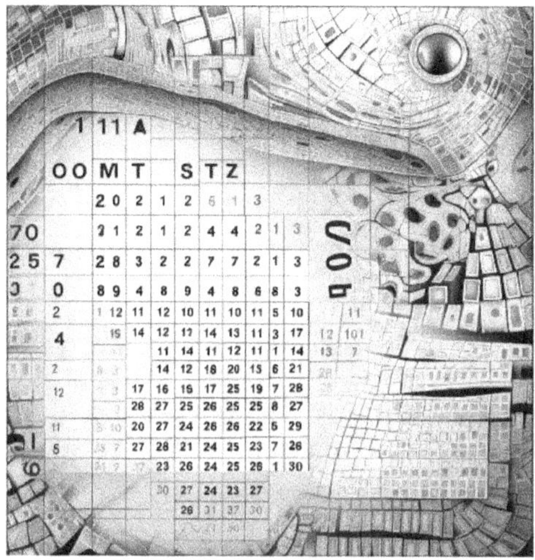

ASTROLOGICAL INFLUENCES

Astrological events can have an impact on your energy levels, emotions and life journey. Here are some significant astrological events to keep an eye on and their potential effects on individuals born under Taurus.

- **Venus Retrograde (January 1. January 29);** At the beginning of the year your ruling planet Venus goes retrograde. This period might encourage you to reassess your relationships and financial matters. Take time to contemplate your values when it comes to love and money.

- **Taurus Season (April 20. May 20);** During Taurus season you will feel more connected to your core traits emphasizing your determination and practicality. You will experience a sense of grounding and focus during this time making it an ideal period for setting goals and pursuing them.

- **Lunar and Solar Eclipse in Taurus (periodic);** A lunar eclipse occurring in your sign may bring about intensity and transformative changes in your life. The eclipse has the potential to bring about transformations, in your life urging you to let go of patterns and embrace personal growth.

- **Retrograde of other Planets (periodic)**; Jupiter, known as the planet of expansion, moves into Pisces. This influences your social life. During this period expect your social circle to expand, providing avenues for spiritual growth through connections with others.

- **Mercury Retrograde (periodic);** Be mindful of Mercury retrogrades that may impact communication and decision making processes at times. Take caution when dealing with contracts or important conversations during these periods. Instead use these times for reflection and review before making any decisions.

Throughout the year Saturn remains in Aquarius putting a spotlight on your career and public life. While you continue to work towards achieving your career goals it's crucial to remain open minded towards innovation and be willing to adapt as changes arise along your path.

KEY AREAS OF CONSIDERATION

LOVE AND RELATIONSHIPS

For Taurus individuals your romantic life and relationships will be influenced by astrological occurrences in the coming year. Pay attention to the following;

- **Venus Retrograde** (January 1. January 29); During this period you may find yourself contemplating relationships and reassessing your values when it comes to love. It's a time for self exploration and gaining insights into your desires.
- **Lunar Eclipse in Taurus (Periodic);** This celestial event holds significance, for matters of the heart. A lunar eclipse has the potential to bring about changes and transformations in your romantic life. It may lead to shifts in your relationships allowing you to let go of patterns and embrace growth.
- **Venus (May 2nd to May 27th);** Venus will grace your sign of Taurus. This period will enhance your qualities and charm creating an opportunity for building or nurturing a deep connection with your partner.

CAREER AND FINANCES

Taurus individuals can expect key events throughout the year that will influence their career and finance. Here are some key moments to keep an eye on.

- **Saturn's presence;** Saturn will continue its presence in Aquarius throughout the year emphasizing your life. Be prepared for work and potential rewards along your career path.

- **Jupiter's transit;** Jupiter's transit through Pisces will focus on friendships and social connections. This period can bring opportunities for career growth through networking and collaborations.
- **Mercury retrograde;** During dates when Mercury goes into retrograde it is advisable to exercise caution with decisions and contracts. Utilize these periods, for review and planning purposes.
- **Mars in Taurus;** During the period of Mars in Taurus, you will find yourself driven and motivated to take on career challenges and financial goals with a sense of determination.

HEALTH AND WELLNESS

Taurus individuals can expect key events throughout the year that will influence their health and wellness. Here are some key moments to keep an eye on.

- **Lunar Eclipse;** When the Lunar Eclipse occurs be prepared for heightened intensity. Use this time to focus on self care and adopt stress management techniques.
- **Venus in Taurus;** An opportunity for indulging in self care and pampering. Make sure you pay attention to both your emotional well being during this period.
- **Saturn;** Throughout the year Saturn will present to remind you of the importance of maintaining a

work life balance. It is crucial not to overwork yourself but prioritize relaxation and rest.

GROWTH AND SELF DISCOVERY

Throughout the year Taurus individuals can leverage astrological events to their advantage. Here are some tips for making the most of what lies ahead.

- **Venus Retrograde;** During Venus Retrograde take time for introspection regarding your values in love and relationships. Use this period as an opportunity to gain an understanding of your desires.
- **Eclipse;** Align with growth and self discovery. Embrace new experiences that resonate with yourself.

As we come to the end of this section we have embarked on a journey through the stars exploring the forces and cosmic energies that will shape the path of Taurus individuals. As you navigate through events and astrological influences always remember that you possess inner strength to overcome obstacles and wisdom to seize opportunities. Your journey in the coming year holds potential for love, success in career well being and personal growth. By staying attuned to influences and being open to change and self discovery you can make the most of opportunities that come your way. Trust in your qualities and ability to adapt and you'll see that the universe supports your efforts.

Remember that astrology can be a tool for self awareness and guidance. It's ultimately your choices and actions that shape your future. As you move forward into the year use the energy of the cosmos to make your dreams come true.

Taurus, this is your chance to shine!

CHAPTER 7:
FAMOUS "TAURUS" PERSONALITIES

In the realm of astrology, the Taurus zodiac sign is often associated with qualities, like determination, practicality, loyalty and a passion for enjoying life's pleasures. People born under Taurus are known for their dedication to their goals and their ability to create stability in their lives. Within this chapter we cordially invite you to explore the lives and accomplishments of famous individuals who share the Taurus star sign. From domains like entertainment, politics, sports and more these famous Taurus personalities have left an imprint on history. In fact they continue to inspire us with their qualities and contributions.

As we dive into the stories of these individuals you will uncover how the traits commonly associated with Taurus have played a role in shaping their path towards success. These icons exemplify the core essence of being a Taurus in diverse and captivating ways. Come along on a journey through their lives as we gain an understanding of how Taurus, astrological influences have shaped their destinies.

ELIZABETH II

- Date of Birth: April 21, 1926.
- Brief Biography: Queen Elizabeth II was the longest-reigning monarch in British history. She ascended to the throne in 1952 and presided over

the United Kingdom and the Commonwealth
with grace and dedication.

- Taurus Traits: Queen Elizabeth II embodied Taurus traits like determination and an unwavering commitment to her royal duties.
- Impact: Her reign witnessed significant historical events, making her a symbol of continuity and stability.
- Personal Life: Queen Elizabeth II was known for her dedication to public service and her close-knit royal family.

BARBRA STREISAND

- Date of Birth: April 24, 1942.
- Brief Biography: Barbra Streisand is an iconic American singer, actress, and filmmaker. She is known for her powerful voice and numerous achievements in the entertainment industry.
- Taurus Traits: Her determination and pursuit of excellence align with Taurus qualities, contributing to her long-lasting success.
- Impact: Streisand has won multiple Grammy Awards, Academy Awards, and Tony Awards for her contributions to entertainment.
- Personal Life: She is also known for her philanthropic efforts and advocacy for various causes.

AUDREY HEPBURN

- Date of Birth: May 4, 1929.
- Brief Biography: Audrey Hepburn was a beloved British actress and humanitarian known for her elegance and grace on and off the screen. She won an Academy Award for her role in "Roman Holiday" and starred in iconic films like "Breakfast at Tiffany's."
- Taurus Traits: Hepburn's determination, poise, and enduring popularity reflect Taurus qualities.
- Impact: She remains an enduring symbol of timeless beauty and style, and her humanitarian work continues to make a positive impact.
- Personal Life: Hepburn was also dedicated to UNICEF and worked tirelessly for children's rights.

MELANIA TRUMP

- Date of Birth: April 26, 1970.
- Brief Biography: Melania Trump is a former First Lady of the United States and a former model. She served as First Lady from 2017 to 2021, focusing on initiatives such as children's well-being and online safety.
- Taurus Traits: Melania Trump's practicality and determination are evident in her approach to her role as First Lady.
- Impact: Her time in the White House saw various initiatives aimed at making a positive impact on society.
- Personal Life: Melania Trump is known for her privacy and her family life with former President Donald Trump.

ADELE

- Date of Birth: May 5, 1988.
- Brief Biography: Adele is a British singer and songwriter known for her soulful and powerful voice. She gained worldwide recognition for her albums, including "21" and "25."
- Taurus Traits: Her determination and practicality are evident in her dedication to her craft and her ability to connect with audiences.
- Impact: Adele has won numerous Grammy Awards and has achieved record-breaking album sales.

- Personal Life: She has been open about her personal experiences, which often inspire her music.

CHER

- Date of Birth: May 20, 1946.
- Brief Biography: Cher is an American singer, actress, and cultural icon known for her versatile career in music and film.
- Taurus Traits: Cher's enduring success and resilience align with Taurus qualities of determination and loyalty.
- Impact: She has won an Academy Award, Grammy Awards, and an Emmy, among other accolades.
- Personal Life: Cher's career has spanned decades, and her personal life has often been in the public eye.

WILLIAM SHAKESPEARE

- Date of Birth: April 26, 1564.
- Brief Biography: William Shakespeare was an English playwright and poet widely regarded as one of the greatest writers in the English language. His works, including "Romeo and Juliet," "Hamlet," and "Macbeth," are considered timeless classics of literature.
- Taurus Traits: Shakespeare's enduring legacy reflects the determination and creativity associated with Taurus.

- Impact: His contributions to literature and the arts have had a profound and enduring influence on culture and language.
- Personal Life: While details of his personal life are limited, his literary achievements continue to inspire generations.

STEVIE WONDER

- Date of Birth: May 13, 1950.
- Brief Biography: Stevie Wonder is an American singer-songwriter, musician, and record producer known for his groundbreaking contributions to music. He has won multiple Grammy Awards and is celebrated for albums like "Songs in the Key of Life."
- Taurus Traits: Stevie Wonder's determination and artistic creativity align with Taurus qualities.
- Impact: His music has touched the hearts of millions and inspired social change through his lyrics and activism.
- Personal Life: Despite blindness from infancy, he has overcome obstacles to become a musical legend.

GEORGE CLOONEY

- Date of Birth: May 6, 1961.
- Brief Biography: George Clooney is an American actor, filmmaker, and philanthropist known for his charm and versatility in Hollywood. He has won Academy Awards as both an actor and a

producer and is known for films like "Ocean's Eleven."

- Taurus Traits: George Clooney's success and commitment to humanitarian causes reflect Taurus qualities.
- Impact: He has used his platform to advocate for various humanitarian efforts and remains a prominent figure in entertainment.
- Personal Life: Clooney is known for his advocacy and his marriage to human rights lawyer Amal Clooney.

POPE JOHN PAUL II (KAROL JOZEF WOJTYLA)

- Date of Birth: May 18, 1920.
- Brief Biography: John Paul II, born Karol Józef Wojtyła, was the head of the Roman Catholic Church as Pope from 1978 until his passing in 2005. He was the second-longest-serving Pope in history and a pivotal figure during the Cold War era.
- Taurus Traits: His steadfast dedication to his role as Pope and his commitment to peace align with Taurus traits like determination and practicality.
- Impact: John Paul II' had a profound impact on the Catholic Church and global politics, earning him recognition as a spiritual leader and advocate for human rights.
- Personal Life: As Pope, his personal life was deeply intertwined with his religious and pastoral duties.

MUSTAFA KEMAL ATATÜRK

- Date of Birth: May 19, 1881.
- Brief Biography: Mustafa Kemal Atatürk, born Mustafa Kemal, was the founder of modern Turkey and its first President. He led sweeping reforms that transformed Turkey into a secular and modern nation-state.
- Taurus Traits: Atatürk's determination to reshape Turkey and his practical approach to nation-building align with Taurus qualities.
- Impact: He is celebrated as a national hero in Turkey and is recognized for his enduring influence on the country's politics, culture, and identity.
- Personal Life: His personal life was deeply tied to his role as a statesman and leader of the Turkish people.

MARK ZUCKERBERG

- Date of Birth: May 14, 1984.
- Brief Biography: Mark Zuckerberg is an American computer programmer and entrepreneur who co-founded Facebook, one of the world's most prominent social media platforms.
- Taurus Traits: His determination, practicality, and steadfast commitment to the growth of Facebook align with Taurus qualities.
- Impact: Facebook has had a profound influence on global connectivity and communication, shaping the way people interact online.

- Personal Life: Zuckerberg is known for his philanthropic efforts and his role as the CEO of Meta Platforms, the parent company of Facebook.

As we wrap up this chapter highlighting individuals born under the Taurus zodiac sign we have embarked on a journey through the lives of individuals who exemplify Taurus traits. From captivating stages in the entertainment industry to positions of power and influence. These individuals have showcased how determination, practicality and loyalty can shape their paths to success.

May the stories of these Taurus figures ignite a sense of inspiration within you to embrace your unique strengths and navigate a path towards personal achievement and fulfillment. Just as constellations illuminate our night sky, so too do Taurus individuals shine brightly with their talents and aspirations continuing to leave a lasting impact on our world.

CONCLUSION

Dear reader, we have reached the conclusion of this book. Together we have embarked on a voyage through the aspects of Taurus delving into its rich history, captivating mythology, distinct traits and the countless ways it shapes the lives of those born under its influence. As we approach the concluding pages of this book let us pause for a moment to reflect on the wisdom and invaluable lessons we have absorbed.

Throughout our exploration we have unraveled the tapestry that's Taurus. We've discovered its origins in history, explored its impact on matters of love and relationships. We have examined its dynamics within friendships and families, analyzed its aspirations in careers and finances. We also delved into its potential for growth and development. Moreover we've celebrated individuals embodying the spirit of Taurus who have left a mark on our world. Now we shall distill these insights into a radiant constellation of knowledge—providing you with a comprehensive overview encapsulating the essence of Taurus!

As we come to the end of our exploration of the Taurus zodiac sign we find ourselves at a crossroads, in the cosmos. Here history, mythology, love, friendships, family, career aspirations, personal growth, future prospects and the influential presence of known Taurus personalities intersect. At this junction of knowledge and awe inspiring wonders we offer you a conclusion that encapsulates the wisdom we have discovered throughout these chapters. Let us summarize what we learned in each.

- **Chapter 1; History and Mythology;** In Chapter 1 we embarked on a captivating journey into the past as we unraveled the origins and legendary tales that shaped the Taurus constellation. From ancient civilizations to enduring myths and legends, Taurus has served as a source of inspiration across countless generations.

- **Chapter 2; Love & Compatibility;** Moving on to Chapter 2 we delved into matters of the heart by exploring how individuals born under the sign of Taurus approach love and relationships. We uncovered insights into their compatibility with zodiac signs—revealing intricate nuances that govern romantic connections guided by its celestial influence.

- **Chapter 3; Friends and Family;** In Chapter 3 we celebrated the cherished roles played by Taurus individuals as friends and family members. We explored their dynamics within relationships while offering insights, into both challenges and rewards found in familial bonds and friendships.

- **Chapter 4; Career and Finance;** In Chapter 4 we delved into the realms of career and finances exploring the preferences, strengths and challenges that Taurus individuals often encounter. We discussed how they strive for stability and achievement through their work ethic.

- **Chapter 5; Self Improvement;** Chapter 5 took us on a journey of self improvement and personal development uncovering how Taurus individuals can utilize their strengths to overcome obstacles and become the versions of themselves.

- **Chapter 6; The Year Ahead;** In Chapter 6 we gazed into the crystal ball to gain insights into what the upcoming year may hold for Taurus individuals. From shifting events in the stars to cosmic guidance we provided a roadmap, for navigating the year ahead.

- **Chapter 7; Famous Taurus Personalities;** Throughout Chapter 7 we celebrated personalities who were born under the Taurus zodiac sign. From Queen Elizabeth II to Mark Zuckerberg, their remarkable journeys shed light on how celestial influences have shaped their lives.

As we conclude this voyage together our hope is that you not only gained a deeper understanding of what it means to be a Taurus but also recognized your limitless potential. The universe has granted you an identity and your journey serves as a testament to the brilliance of the cosmos itself.

To all our readers born under the sign of Taurus we extend words of encouragement. Embrace your qualities with pride and conviction. Your traits serve as guiding stars illuminating your extraordinary journey forward. Your individual cosmic identity holds a wellspring of strength, creativity and resilience. As you navigate through the changing landscape of life, always remember that the universe has bestowed upon you remarkable gifts.

In the spirit of unity and appreciation, for the zodiac we encourage individuals from all signs to embrace and celebrate their qualities. Like each constellation in the night sky possesses its brilliance, so do our individual qualities and traits that define us. Within this tapestry every star radiates its own light contributing to the beauty and wonder of our universe.

As we say our goodbyes, may you continue exploring the enigmas of the universe finding inspiration in constellations above and embracing possibilities. The cosmos is your guiding force and your journey has only just begun. Throughout this odyssey we have ventured into realms of Taurus zodiac sign uncovering its secrets and celebrating its characteristics. As we reflect upon our expedition let us distill the essence of our exploration once again to reaffirm our commitment and offer a guiding star to illuminate your path.

We embarked on this expedition with a pledge to unravel Taurus' rich tapestry. From its origins to its impact on love, family dynamics, career paths and personal growth. We have fulfilled our promise by providing a range of insights, guidance and inspiration to help you navigate the twists and turns of life. Our mission was to shed light on your journey of self discovery. We have accomplished that by revealing the map that defines your Taurus identity.

If there's one thing we hope you take away from this book, it's the importance of self awareness and the timeless enchantment of astrology. Embrace your qualities whether you belong to Taurus or any other zodiac sign. Utilize the wisdom of the stars to navigate through this cosmic voyage.

The characteristics of Taurus, determination, loyalty and practicality have undeniably made a mark on humanity's tapestry. As you move forward may the stars remain as your guiding lights. May you forever draw inspiration from the marvels that envelop us. Embrace your identity and let the magnificence of the cosmos illuminate your path on this remarkable journey we call life.

www.ingramcontent.com/pod-product-compliance
Lightning Source LLC
Chambersburg PA
CBHW050601160726
48003CB00002B/999